WHY IS MY HOUSE ALWAYS A Mess?

WHY IS MY HOUSE ALWAYS A Mess?

How to Declutter & Organize Your Home in Just 30 Days

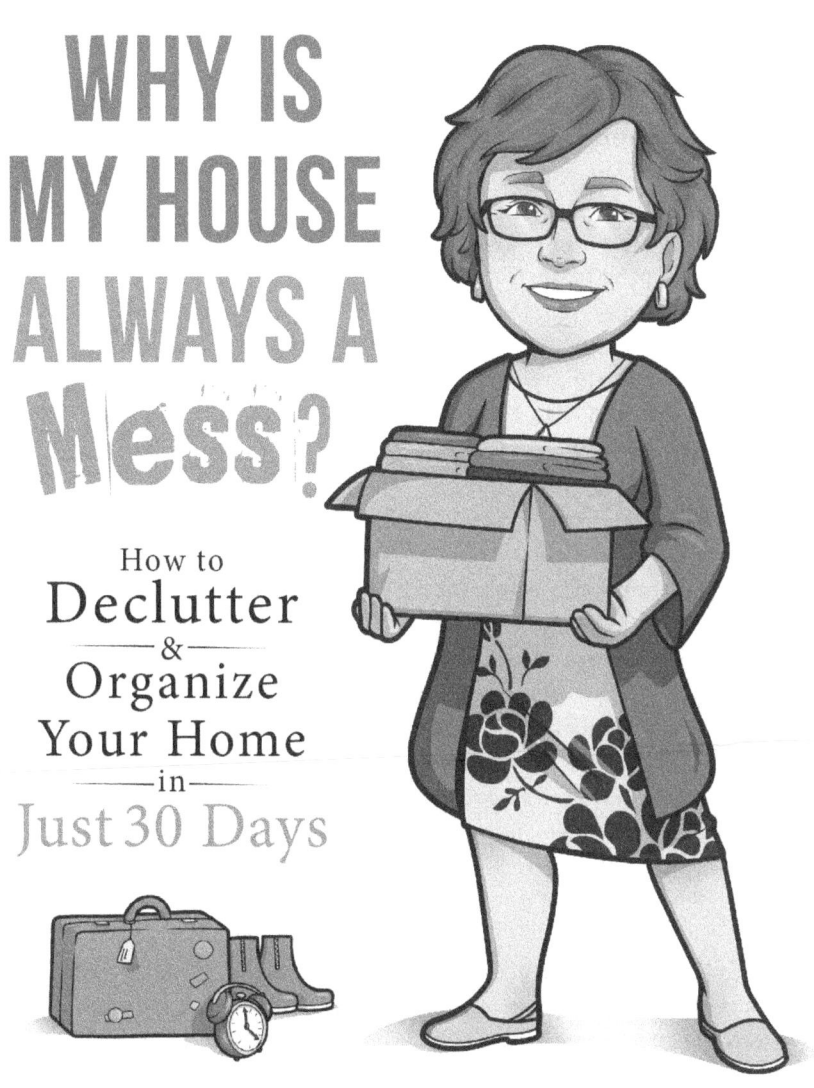

JOANNE "GRAM" RADKE

Copyright © 2024 Joanne Radke.

All Rights Reserved. No portion of this book may be reproduced in any form without permission from the publisher except as permitted by U.S. copyright law. For permissions, contact: joanne.p.radke@gmail.com

Cover illustration by Love Pixels
Cover Design by Tehsin Gul
Interior design by Amit Dey

ISBN: 979-8-89419-512-4 (sc)
ISBN: 979-8-89419-513-1 (hc)
ISBN: 979-8-89419-514-8 (e)

All scriptures are from THE HOLY BIBLE, NEW INTERNATIONAL VERSION®. Copyright© 1973, 1978, 1984, 2011 by Biblica, Inc.™. Used by permission of Zondervan.

Disclaimer: Although the author has made every effort to ensure that the information in this book was correct at press time, and while this publication is designed to provide accurate information in regard to the subject matter covered, "the author" assumes no responsibility for errors, inaccuracies, omissions, or any other inconsistencies herein and hereby disclaims any liability to any party for any loss, damage, or disruption caused by errors or omissions, whether such errors or omissions result from negligence, accident, or any other cause.

This publication is meant as a source of valuable information for the reader. However, it is not meant as a substitute for direct expert assistance. If such a level of assistance is required, the services of a competent professional should be sought.

One Galleria Blvd., Suite 1900, Metairie, LA 70001
(504) 702-6708

DEDICATION

I dedicate this book to my Mom and Dad, Art, and Vi Radke. Dad, the Hoarder in the family, and Mom, the Clean Freak, taught me well.

I am looking forward to seeing you both again on the other side.

I also dedicate this book to my dear brother Dave, a blessing and friend, I love dearly. I have learned so many lessons from all three.

Thank you all so much for what you have poured into my life all these years to make me who and what I am today. Love you. PP Jo

TABLE OF CONTENTS

Introduction xiii

The Daily Format xvii

Day 1: Setting Spiritual Foundations for Decluttering 1

Day 2: Praying for a Decluttered Home and Heart 9

Day 3: Decluttering Your Mindset Embracing Simplicity 17

Day 4: Cultivating Gratitude in the Decluttering Process 23

Day 5: Seeking God's Guidance in Decision Making. 29

Day 6: Decluttering Your Physical Environment. Where do I Begin? . 37

Day 7: The Importance of Decluttering Sentimental Items 45

Day 8: Creating a Decluttering Schedule and Routine 51

Day 9: Organizing and Decluttering Your Closet 57

Day 10: Simplifying your Wardrobe: Finding Joy in Less 63

Day 11: Decluttering and Organizing Kitchen Spaces 69

Day 12: Embracing Minimalism in the Kitchen 75

Day 13: Decluttering and Organizing Living Spaces 81

Day 14: Creating a Cozy and Clutter-Free Living Room 87
Day 15: Decluttering Digital Space Managing Technology 93
Day 16: Tackling Paper Clutter Managing Documents and Mail . . .99
Day 17: Organizing and Simplifying your Home Office or Workspace . 105
Day 18: Decluttering and Streamlining Your Cleaning Routine . . . 111
Day 19: Decluttering and Organizing Children's Spaces 117
Day 20: Teaching Children the Value of Simplicity. 123
Day 21: Decluttering and Organizing My Bathroom and Toiletries . 129
Day 22: Creating a Restful and Decluttered Bedroom 135
Day 23: Decluttering and Organizing the Garage and Storage Areas . . 141
Day 24: Simplifying Home Décor Finding Beauty in Simplicity . . . 147
Day 25: Letting Go of Cluttered Relationships and Boundaries . . . 153
Day 26: Decluttering Your Time Prioritizing and Saying No 161
Day 27: The Benefits of Decluttering for Mental and Emotional Well-Being. 167
Day 28: Maintaining a Decluttered Home Habits and Systems. . . . 173
Day 29: Celebrating Progress and Overcoming Decluttering Challenges. 179
Day 30 : Reflecting on the Spiritual Lessons Learned in this Decluttering Journey. 185

Acknowledgments. 191
About the Author 193
Other Books and Material by Joanne Radke. 195
Were You Blessed?. 197

THANK YOU !

I would like to thank you, my reader, for picking this book up to help you on your decluttering journey.

As a thank you, I would like to send you via your e-mail my Cluttering Free Newsletter. In the first edition, you can sign up and become a member of our Clutter Free Club, where we will offer more tips and suggestions for getting your home totally clutter-free.

For more training, tips and special offers, sign up now for your free Clutter Free Newsletter.

Just visit: Gift.Declutterin30Days.com

INTRODUCTION

Do you ever feel out of control? Overwhelmed? Hopeless? Are you wondering how you ever got here or how you will ever get back control of your life? Ever wonder when the world is going to stop and let you off? Have no fear. Hope is here!

Your life, like mine, is divided into many sections and areas: your home, work, family, kids, other relationships, finances, body, soul, and spirit. It is very easy to lump them all together, and when we do that, we become overwhelmed, like you feel now, right?

Yes, I hear you! I have been there many times, especially in the early days of my adult life. Then hope came by and rescued me. Hope can rescue you as well.

One day, someone came into my life, by accident really, to help me and show me 'How to Take Back Control of my Life.' And initially, it only took me 30 days to get started and get into the habit of decluttering and organizing. That is all it will take for you as well. Just 30 days to make the habit and continue your life of organizing and decluttering. One step at a time, starting NOW!

Over these almost 70 years, I have learned that life is hard and not easy by myself. Being overwhelmed with my life became my middle name: *"Joanne Overwhelmed."* Now that doesn't sound right, but that was how I felt.

This was one place I didn't want to be, so how was I going to get out of this situation and the feeling of being so overwhelmed? I was tired and confused, needing help fast. Who can I turn to?

That help came in the form of a friend. Life is so much easier and better when you have a friend to help you along the way. Wouldn't you agree? So let me be your friend and help you take back control of your life by "Taking Back Control of Your House" to start with and helping you to declutter your home.

Walk with me through this 30-day practical guide to decluttering and organizing your house, and watch your life change forever as you change your house of chaos into a home of peace.

Sound good? Let's get started!

THE DAILY FORMAT

Let's begin by sharing each day's topic and devotional format.

Each day, we will begin with an inspirational quote to encourage you along the way, followed by scripture to help you seek God's guidance on your decluttering journey.

Next comes the training pertaining to each day's topic, followed by a prayer asking God to help us on this adventure.

Each day, we will have a question(s) to ask you to keep you motivated on this decluttering journey. Answer them as honestly as you can before you go on to the next day.

Finally, we will end with an affirmation to affirm to your mind and heart that you are determined to move forward on this daily adventure. This is to inspire and challenge you on your spiritual and physical decluttering journey.

I hope this devotional course on decluttering your home will get you thinking and open you to new ideas and ways of doing things.

I pray that it will bless you and inspire you to keep growing in this area of your life and, when you are done, continue conquering all the clutter that dares come your way.

Your first action item, even before you begin, would be to get yourself a journal, a 3-ring binder, or something to write in day by day, as this will inspire you when you are struggling.

Every day, may I encourage you to write down what you are feeling and learning and reflect on it as you go along. Have fun, and may God bless you as you declutter your home.

Sincerely,

Joanne "Gram" Radke

DAY 1

SETTING SPIRITUAL FOUNDATIONS FOR DECLUTTERING

Nate Berkus once said, "Your home should tell the story of who you are and be a collection of what you love."

Today's Bible Verse

Jesus looked at them and said, "With man this is impossible, but with God all things are possible." Matthew 19:26.

What better path to take than one found in the Word of God in the Bible? God has a plan for us, and He clearly shows us what that path is if we take the time to read it and search for it with all our hearts.

What better way to start this new adventure than by inviting God, our greatest organizer, into the process with us.

I grew up with a dad who was a hoarder and became one myself. I was never as bad as he was, but I was a hoarder just the same. What can I say? I loved my stuff and had a hard time parting with any of it. I would rationalize to myself, "I can't throw it away. When I throw it away, I may need it."

How would I change and help myself become more organized when I had this difficult lineage in my background? I had a lot to overcome. I needed new eyes to see the beauty of order and the chaos of my clutter.

I needed a new mindset, a new way of thinking about stuff. I needed a new set of glasses to see the clutter and a new heart to let go of what I was holding on to. Only God could help me do that.

Letting go is so hard as we become attached to our things without even realizing why. Sometimes, it is sentimental, and sometimes, it's emotional or even psychological.

We must stop and think about why we find it hard to let go and ask the Lord to show us why we are attached to all our stuff. Are you willing to do that? Why?

Take a few moments now and write down your thoughts.

"What is the reason and motivation that makes me hang onto my stuff?"

_____
_____
_____
_____
_____
_____
_____
_____
_____
_____

When we find the root of the attachments, we can let go of them and continue our healing journey of decluttering and organizing. Only then will we be able to declutter much easier and 'LET GO' much quicker of the things we hold on to.

The Lord wants to give us the hope and strength to help us change and walk into our new freedom of order and peace. So, there is hope for you.

If I can change with God's help, so can you. Amen. Yes, you can!

Just commit this process and your house to the Lord for the next 30 days and watch Him work in your life and heart, changing your mindset toward stuff and helping you move forward, one day at a time. God will light your path on this journey of discovery.

What lurks in the dark corners of your home? Want to look, and see? Choose to trust Him even when anxious about what to keep and give away.

Write how you are feeling below.

_____
_____
_____
_____
_____
_____
_____

Set aside 15 minutes every day to declutter a specific area of your house. If you need more time, take it. Start with a small area like a drawer or a closet and work up to a room layout.

Track your progress in your journal. Like this. Today, I cleaned out the kitchen drawer and found my _____, which I hadn't seen in 2.5 years.

Daily Prayer

Heavenly Father, thank You for guiding and directing me on this decluttering and organizing journey. I certainly can't do it on my own. I have tried and failed terribly. Help me to create a space that reflects your love and order. I pray for Your joy to fill my heart as I release the excess and create a home of order and peace. Thank you, Father. In Jesus' name, I pray, Amen.

Questions

"What does it mean for me to declutter my home?" Write down your answer.

"Am I committed to creating a clutter-free, organized home reflecting my true self?"

Affirmation

"I am committed to creating a clutter-free and organized home that reflects my true self."

Notes, Ideas, Thoughts & Prayers

DAY 2

PRAYING FOR A DECLUTTERED HOME AND HEART

Lao Tzu once said, "The journey of a thousand miles begins with a single step." So, start one step at a time, and before you know it, you will be at the finish line.

Today's Bible Verse

"Do not be anxious about anything, but in every situation, by prayer and petition, with thanksgiving, present your requests to God. And the peace of God, which transcends all understanding, will guard your hearts and minds in Christ Jesus." Philippians 4:6-7

As you give this journey to God, give Him all your fear and worry. Ask Him for His wisdom and guidance as to where to start and what to do next, and let His peace keep you as you go day by day, decluttering your stuff.

Yes, we are on a journey. The hardest part is getting started, so let's get to it and create a plan. Why not try one room at a time? Pick a room. Any room.

- What needs to be removed and decluttered in this room?
- What needs to be organized in this room?
- What needs to be cleaned in this room? Write your answers below.

_____

_____

_____

_____

_____

Remember, just 15 minutes here and 15 minutes there, every 15 minutes adds up, and before you know it, your room is clean and decluttered.

This is how I started so many years ago. My Mom said, "Jo, clean up your room!" I asked, "How?" Mom said, "Like this!" She showed me how by doing it herself. That only worked for a few days, and then she left me to my own devices. She knew how to clean and organize and put everything in its place. She was a clean freak. She taught me by example, and she gave me motivation.

Make a plan and stick with it. When the plan doesn't work, tweak it and try it again. Eventually, your plan will work. Write out your plan. Put it in your journal and tweak it when you need to. Your plan will lead to action. Your action will lead to accomplishment. Your accomplishment will lead to an organized space and peace and rest. You can do this!

Make a plan, room by room, of how you want to declutter and organize your house. "One room at a time, dear Jesus, that's all I'm asking of you!"

Begin each decluttering session with a prayer, asking God to help you by giving you His wisdom and ability to let go of the things you don't need or want anymore.

Daily Prayer

As I begin this journey, God, help me embrace each step with enthusiasm and gratitude. Help me to find joy in this process as I celebrate the progress, I accomplish each day. Thank you that I am not alone in this but that Your presence continues to fill me, giving me the strength to keep going. Fill my mind with Your wisdom and peace and my spirit with Your joy as I declutter my home with You by my side. In Jesus' name, I pray. Amen"

Questions

"Am I open to God's help in my decluttering process?"

Think about it and write your answer below before beginning day 3.

_____
_____
_____
_____
_____
_____
_____
_____
_____
_____
_____

Affirmation

"I am open to divine guidance as I declutter my home and create a harmonious living space."

Notes, Ideas, Thoughts & Prayers

DAY 3

DECLUTTERING YOUR MINDSET EMBRACING SIMPLICITY

Leonardo da Vinci once said, "Simplicity is the ultimate sophistication."

Today's Bible Verse

> "Do not store up for yourselves treasures on earth, where moths and vermin destroy, and where thieves break in and steal. But store up for yourselves treasures in heaven, where moths and vermin do not destroy, and where thieves do not break in and steal. For where your treasure is, there your heart will be also." Matthew 6:19-21

When you think about it, most of us have a mountain of stuff to go through right now, and that thought is already too overwhelming. And to that, the easy access to shopping online and having anything we want or need on our doorstep in less than 24 hours multiplies the problem.

Have you ever asked yourself this question: "How many bags or boxes of stuff do I bring in my home every day compared to how many bags or boxes of stuff I take out?"

If the bags you bring into your home are more than those you remove, you have a problem. Soon, you will be overwhelmed again with too much stuff and must go through the decluttering process again. Something we need to keep in mind.

Let's think about why we buy and need so much stuff before we can tackle the decluttering question or problem. Think about it and write your comments below. "Do I have a problem with needing to buy more stuff, clothes, etc., to satisfy a need in my heart?"

Ask God, your creator, to show you if you have a problem. Where did it come from? Was your mother, father, or sister a compulsive shopper? Write down your answers.

Let's take Matthew 6:19-21 to heart and ask God to help us not to store up treasures on this earth. We need to ask God to help us let go of our stuff and give some of it away to those who don't have it and can't afford it, to those who can use it. If we do this, we will start the letting go process and feel good about helping many less fortunate people.

We certainly can learn from those around us who are minimalists. They only have what they need and give everything else away to others who can use it.

Daily Prayer

Father God, forgive me for being a hoarder of stuff, storing up my treasure on earth. Would you show me where this bondage came from and help me to overcome it with the Holy Spirit's help. Help me let go of the things I don't need or use. Help me to be willing to give it away joyfully to those who can't afford it or who could use it. Please help me to look more like Heavenly Father, generous and kind. In Jesus' name, Amen.

Questions

"Where does my mindset need to change to embrace simplicity?"

Think about it and write your answer below before beginning day 4.

_____

_____

_____

_____

_____

"Where does my mindset need to change to achieve this goal of sharing with others?"

_____

_____

_____

_____

_____

_____

Affirmation

"I embrace simplicity and let go of my possessions that no longer serve me, creating space for what truly matters."

Notes, Ideas, Thoughts & Prayers

DAY 4

CULTIVATING GRATITUDE IN THE DECLUTTERING PROCESS

Did you know that "Gratitude turns what we have into enough."
- Anonymous

Today's Bible Verse

"Give thanks in all circumstances; for this is God's will for you in Christ Jesus." 1 Thessalonians 5:18

Did you ever stop and think how powerful gratitude is? It is a force that opens doors to opportunity and blessing. Did you know we spend half our life striving to get ahead and the other half complaining about the process?

If we stopped long enough to listen to what we say, we would want to change our thinking, attitude, and hearts.

Stop and listen to your talk, your thoughts. Most are negative and complaining. That is human nature. Oh, how our lives would be so different by one simple change: being thankful instead of staying ungrateful.

Throughout this decluttering challenge, we must start practicing the 3 G Process.

1. **Gratitude**
   Be grateful and thank God for his provision in your life, for the family and friends who gave you all your stuff, gifts, etc., that you enjoy.

2. **Grace**
   Ask God for His supernatural grace to let go of your stuff graciously and joyfully.

3. **Giving**
   Ask God to give you His heart for others, to give your stuff away to the less fortunate with a joyful heart.

Start looking at the stuff you want to give away. "One man's junk is another man's treasure." Your heart will be full as you think about and anticipate their joy when they receive their new treasures.

Practice gratitude by decluttering what you don't need and focusing on appreciating the essentials that bring you true joy and contentment. Practice gratitude each day by being thankful for three items you have in your home.

Daily Prayer

Heavenly Father, would you give me a heart of gratitude and thanksgiving each day. Help me to be thankful for Your provision and presence in my home and my life. Let Your joy be my strength as I walk this decluttering journey with you. May my home be a place of gratitude and contentment where Your love and blessings reside every day. In Jesus' name, I pray. Amen."

Questions

"What are three things I am grateful for today?" Write them below before you go on to day 5.

1.

2.

3.

Affirmation

"I am grateful for the blessings of my home, and I find joy in decluttering and organizing."

DAY 5

SEEKING GOD'S GUIDANCE IN DECISION MAKING

Today's Bible Verses

"Your word is a lamp to my feet, a light to my path." Psalm 119:105

"Trust in the Lord with all your heart and lean not on your own understanding; in all your ways submit to him, and he will make your paths straight." Proverbs 3:5-6

God has you in whatever you must face today. It may seem impossible for you, but if you give that burden and care to Him, He can fix it. He's got you and will make your paths straight. Even on this decluttering journey.

I like and use the three-box method myself. When I start any decluttering project, I take three boxes or three areas in a room. I mark one box or area. 'Things to keep', a second box or area, 'Things to give away or Sell', and a third area or box, 'Things to get rid of for garbage'.

1. **Keep,**
2. **Give Away, or Sell**
3. **Garbage.**

Whatever I declutter, whether a drawer, closet, or room, I use this method, which works well for me. I take an object, look at it, and then ask myself, when was the last time I used or needed it? I then ask God to help me put it in the right box or category.

Do I keep it, do I give it away, or do I throw it away? When I let God help me, I usually stick to that decision. It is important to fill a box or bag, then take it out of the room, ready for the giveaway or garbage bin. Otherwise, it is too big of a temptation to take it back and change my mind. It is also important to release the item from your psyche.

It is okay to say to the item, "Thank you for letting me use you and helping me during this time, but now it is time to say goodbye so that you can become someone else's treasure."

When we say goodbye to our items, we are emotionally letting go of them, and it is easier to release them and no longer have any attachment to them. We will then feel the joy of letting it go and giving it away to someone else who can use it.

It is so easy to go back on your decisions, especially if you don't immediately get the filled box out of your house. When an item stays in your home too long, there is a good chance that when you look at it again, you will drag it out of the box and want to keep it. I have done this several times in my life.

A couple of years ago, I had friends help me declutter my garage, where I had stored much of my house clutter. We spent one Saturday going through the stuff, putting things in my garbage bin and their truck to take to the local thrift store. In the end, it worked well.

When they left with the last load of the giveaway stuff to the thrift store, my garage was so clean you could get two cars in it again. I felt free from the clutter and so full of joy that I finally had a clean garage.

I did regret that I got rid of some of my pictures and some of my music (that I hadn't looked at or listened to for several years), and

I had to deal with that as a loss, which can happen occasionally. It is a part of you or your past that you are losing by choice but losing just the same. The Lord is the only one who can comfort your soul during this time. Forgive yourself for letting it go and making you sad, then get over it.

So, we do need to stick to our choices and let go of our regrets. It is important to go with the flow of God's guidance in your decluttering journey.

It may help to reflect and meditate on today's scripture verses, Proverbs 3:5-6 each day and seek God's guidance in decluttering, as He is much wiser than we are.

Daily Prayer

Father, I trust You as I continue this decluttering journey. Help me to let go of the past and embrace the present with a joyful and grateful heart. Help me to know what to keep and what to let go of with a grateful heart so I can learn that You do all things well. Remind me that each item I release represents a new opportunity to walk in your joy and freedom. In Jesus' name, I pray. Amen."

Questions

"Have I asked God today what I can keep?" Write your answers before you go on to day 6.

"Have I asked God today what I can give away or sell?"

"Have I asked God today what I need to throw away?"

If you haven't asked God, ask Him now. Please write it down and wait to hear what he says before you go on to day 6.

Affirmation

"I trust in the Lord's guidance as I make decisions about what to keep and let go of in my home."

Notes, Ideas, Thoughts & Prayers

DAY 6

DECLUTTERING YOUR PHYSICAL ENVIRONMENT. WHERE DO I BEGIN?

Magdalena Vanden Berg once said, "Clear your clutter, clear your mind."

Today's Bible Verse

"Create in me a pure heart, O God, and renew a steadfast spirit within me." Psalm 51:10

Many people who come to the end of their decluttering journey agree with Magdalena. Now that the clutter is gone, they can think much more clearly.

A play was written by a Salvation Army Officer couple, Major & Mrs. Robert Redhead, who called the play 'The White Rose'. It was the story of a poor family in the heart of London, England. The husband was an abusive alcoholic, and the wife survived by a thread. Their home was messy and in ruins because of the alcohol.

One day, a Salvation Army woman came for a visit and brought a beautiful white rose she gave the wife. The white rose was so beautiful that the wife couldn't find the right place to put it down because her home was in such a terrible mess. After the Salvation Army gal left her home, the wife cleaned up a bit. She cleaned off her table and did her dishes, put a tablecloth on the table, and set the white rose in the vase on the table, then felt motivated to clean the rest of the kitchen and her living room.

When her husband got home, he couldn't get over the change in the house, so he asked her what had happened. She shared with him that the Salvation Army woman came with a white rose, which looked so out of place that she didn't have any place to put it, so she had to clean up so it would fit in.

All it took was one white rose to change their environment. That Sunday, they both went to church and gave their lives to Jesus, which changed them forever.

Is there anything in your life that feels out of place or needs to change? Why not write it below and ask the Lord to create a clean heart and renew a steadfast spirit in you? Just think of what can change and how much more peace you will have if you do that. You will be glad you did.

_____

_____

_____

_____

_____

_____

_____

_____

_____

Making a peaceful place to learn the art of resting in God and changing your mindset is important. Mess breeds mess and unrest, whereas cleanliness breeds peace and rest.

Why not create a designated space in your home, such as a prayer corner or a quiet reading nook, where you can focus on your spiritual inner growth and connection with God?

Why not start decluttering in the cleanest room of your house so you'll get that room done faster, which will motivate you to keep going?

Now, pick another less cluttered room and go for it, continuing to use the three-box method. Now you have another room done. Way to go! Now, commit to decluttering one small area daily, such as a drawer or a shelf. You will be glad you did.

Daily Prayer

Loving God, I come to You with a desire for simplicity and peace in my home. As I declutter, I ask for strength to let go of possessions that no longer serve a purpose in my life. Let me enjoy simplicity and appreciate the blessings of living with less. Help me to create a place for you in my life even more. In Jesus' name, I pray, Amen.

Questions

"What area or room do I want to tackle first?" Think about your home. The drawers, the closet, my bedroom, my kitchen, my entranceway, my office?"

Write your answers before you go on to day 7.

_____
_____
_____
_____
_____

"What area needs to be decluttered? What is in my way, stopping me from starting?"

_____
_____
_____
_____
_____

Pick one and go with it. Write down the room you picked and the reason why you picked that room.

_____
_____
_____
_____
_____

Affirmation

"With each item I declutter, I create more space for peace, clarity, and abundance in my life."

DAY 7

THE IMPORTANCE OF DECLUTTERING SENTIMENTAL ITEMS

William Morris once said, "Have nothing in your houses that you do not know to be useful or believe to be beautiful."

Today's Bible Verse

"Whatever you do, work at it with all your heart, as working for the Lord not human masters." Colossians 3:23

We all have keepsakes or special items with sentimental meaning and value. Your treasures are important to keep and highlight in your home. When you are decluttering, put your sentimental treasures in a separate box or display case for all to see, as they have special significance to you and your family.

For me, I keep them in two different display cases. One is for my mother and her side of the family, and the other is for my father and his family. It isn't necessary to keep everything from your mother or father but rather keep a couple of highlights from their lives.

Both my mom and dad have passed on, so I have little mementos that remind me of them and their side of the family. For my father's display case, I have a picture of when he was small on the homestead, my grandfather's pocket knife, a pair of glasses, a CNCP ID card where dad used to work, a passport picture of my Dad's father, my grandfather, when he came over from the old country and a letter I sent my dad when I was nine when he was in the hospital.

My mother's display case looks very different. I have a picture of mom standing outside her house at 3 years of age, her grandfather's pocket Gideon New Testament, a heart locket, a pair of old glasses, a case, a war ration card from the 2nd World War, and a letter she sent me when I was 20.

Your sentimental treasures are important to keep and highlight. Make a treasure box or special case for your sentimental items. There is no need to keep everything; one or two per person is more than enough.

Choose one sentimental item per person and look for a special way to put it on display. Look online, see how others display their sentimental items, and do the same for you. This could be a good time to share with the family why the item is important and use it to reflect on the blessing that person has given to each of you in your family.

Daily Prayer

Heavenly Father, thank You for the precious memories I have that are attached to these sentimental items in my home. Teach me to cherish these items in meaningful ways while letting go of the items that are no longer needed or bringing me joy. I want my home to be where cherished memories are celebrated, and new memories are created. In Jesus' name, I pray. Amen."

Questions

"What sentimental items do I want to keep and why?"

Write your answers before you go on to day 8.

"What am I going to do to display them in an honoring way?"

You can also take pictures of them and make a scrapbook if there are many. Then, you can pack them up and store them in your storage area.

Think about them and write your thoughts below before you begin Day 8.

Affirmation

"I cherish the sentimental items that truly bring me joy and find creative ways to honor their significance."

Notes, Ideas, Thoughts & Prayers

DAY 8

CREATING A DECLUTTERING SCHEDULE AND ROUTINE

"One small positive thought in the morning can change your whole day." Unknown

Today's Bible Verse

Ecclesiastes 3:1, "There is a time for everything, and a season for every activity under the heavens." Ecclesiastes 3:1

The habit of thinking happy thoughts will keep us on the right track for that day and all our lives if we continue to think happy thoughts every day.

Another good habit is learning to pick up after yourself. That is a habit that will not only bless you but also everyone you live with each day. It is one habit you will be glad to learn for the rest of your life.

Routine is a good thing to keep us focused and productive. What would we do without a routine? We would be like a ship without a sail, tossed to and fro, going in no real direction.

Having a routine for cleaning and decluttering is a good thing, too. To wake up every morning knowing what you will do will keep you on track, focused, and productive. How do you schedule your time every day, every week, every morning, noon, and night? Write it below to keep it in your mind.

_____

_____

_____

_____

_____

_____

A new habit takes 21 days to learn, so making a schedule and letting it become your new routine will help keep your home neat and organized for the rest of your life.

Today, we want to establish a decluttering schedule, dedicating specific days and times for organizing the different areas of your home.

This is a time to establish a weekly routine cleaning schedule for you and your family. If you have children, you must set up a decluttering and cleaning time for them to clean and tidy their rooms.

You will have to go through everything they own with them, so they don't throw everything out, as they may get carried away with the excitement. This is a good time to teach them about the value of things and giving to others and those who don't have as much as they do. How wonderful that would be.

Daily Prayer

Father, I pray for strength and perseverance as I establish a decluttering routine for my family. Please guide me in prioritizing my time and energy to create a plan and a routine for an organized and clutter-free home. Give me discipline and motivation to tackle the tasks at hand. Bless me with the ability to maintain an orderly environment that brings peace and joy to all my family and friends who visit. In Jesus' name, I pray. Amen.

Questions

"What is my weekly and daily cleaning and decluttering schedule."

Think about it and write below before you start day 9. Remember if it isn't quite right you can always tweak it and start again.

_____

_____

_____

_____

_____

_____

_____

_____

_____

Affirmation

"I establish a consistent decluttering routine that brings order, simplicity, and calmness into my home."

Notes, Ideas, Thoughts & Prayers

DAY 9

ORGANIZING AND DECLUTTERING YOUR CLOSET

Today's Bible Verse

"Keep your lives free from the love of money and be content with what you have, because God has said, 'Never will I leave you; never will I forsake you.'" Hebrews 13:5

While in college, my dorm room was immaculate. The House Leader would show off my room as the cleanest, neatest, ideal dorm room. I feared the house leader would one day open my closet door and see my true self, cluttered and disorganized.

Over the years, I have developed my closet obsession: The need to keep it so clean that anyone can visit, go into my closet, and not be shocked that I am a closet messy.

Remember my observation that every bag of stuff you bring into your home needs a bag of stuff to be removed for you to keep on an even keel. Otherwise, your room and home will become cluttered once again.

When decluttering a closet, take everything out of it, every little thing, just as if you are moving in for the first time. Pile all your clothes on top of your bed and your shoes on the floor.

Look at and go through your clothes. Try everything on to see what fits and what you feel good in. Put these in the keep pile. Anything that doesn't fit anymore, or you don't feel good in, can go to the thrift store or the needy. Anything stained, ripped, etc., can go in the rag bag or garbage.

This would also be a good time to re-organize your closet. You can get a custom-made closet organizer organized with the right amount of space, boxes, etc., that is what you want before you start filling it up again. You can purchase many closet units at Ikea, Amazon, Walmart, etc., or have one installed by Home Depot.

I got a bottom rod to hang from the top rung to make an extra rod to hang twice as many things in the same space. Tops on top and slacks on bottom, giving me twice as much closet space. This made a huge difference in my closet and organization.

A dear friend of mine shared this secret with me. When you re-organize your closet, hang every hanger the same way.

Now, when you wear an item, put it back in the closet and put the hanger the other way around. That way, 6 months to a year from now, you will see what pieces of clothing you did and didn't wear in that frame.

Take the clothes you didn't wear, those with the hangers still pointing the way you put them in the closet when you decluttered and give them away. What you haven't worn in 6 months to a year you don't need. Rejoice; you have just found new space to spread out again in your closet.

Now, plan to only put back in the closet things that fit you and you feel good in. Sort by color for easy picking. Now do the same with your shoes, belts, scarves, ties, etc. Most people will have fewer clothes to put back than when they started.

We typically have so much more than we need, so this is a good time to downsize your closet and give those in need the items you don't want. Start each session by decluttering one item causing you stress or anxiety. Sort through your closet and donate at least five items of clothing that you no longer wear. This will start you on a better track. The last time I did this, I gave away 20 pairs of dress pants.

Daily Prayer

Lord, I thank You for the joy of rediscovering forgotten treasures and cherished memories during the decluttering process. May each item I encounter bring a smile to my face and gratitude to my heart. Thank you for helping me with this adventure. In Jesus' name. Amen.

Questions

"What is hiding in my closet that I don't want to look at or tackle?"

Think about it and write it down before you start day 10.

_____

_____

_____

_____

_____

_____

Affirmation

"I approach decluttering with enthusiasm and focus, knowing that each small step brings me closer to my goal."

Notes, Ideas, Thoughts & Prayers

DAY 10

SIMPLIFYING YOUR WARDROBE: FINDING JOY IN LESS

Today's Bible Verse

"But seek first his kingdom and his righteousness, and all these things will be given to you as well." Matthew 6:33

In my 20s, I lived with a friend for a couple of months. She was a beautiful girl studying to be a nurse while working in an agricultural college, tending to the animals. She lived very simply and minimally. She had a dress, a blazer/jacket, a couple of tops, a pair of pants, and a pair of jeans. She always dressed well, but to my shock, she only had a simple wardrobe. Clothes were not her priority. She learned how to mix and match her clothes and did well with just a few pieces. I was amazed.

I lived on a shoestring budget, so I didn't want to throw anything out as I valued what I purchased over the years. For the most part, I wore a uniform, so I didn't need many civilian clothes, yet I had so many more pieces of clothing than my friend did.

I had 8 white blouses, two uniforms, jeans, dress slacks, tops, jackets, scarves, etc. I had a dress, a suitcase of clothes that fit now, clothes that fit last year in hopes of losing weight, and clothes that would fit if I gained a bit along the way. When I came to my senses several years later, I got rid of most of my suitcases of clothes as they either still didn't fit or they were out of style. It would have been better if I had given them away at the time and let someone else be able to wear them rather than have them sit in a suitcase or the back of my closet.

What do you have in your closet? And what should we have in our closets?

_____

_____

_____

_____

_____

We should have clothes that we can mix and match together.

A WOMAN'S WARDROBE

For example, for women, here is a simple list.

- 5-7 tops in different colors
- 5-7 jackets in different styles and colors
- 1 little black dress
- 3 dresses
- 4 skirts in 4 different colors
- 4 slacks in 4 different colors
- 1 pair of jeans
- 4 pairs of shoes: a pair of running shoes, a comfy pair, office dress shoes, and pumps

This amount will give you 50 to 75 different outfits through mixing and matching together. Enough for 2.5 months without wearing the same thing twice. You can downsize and still have a fabulous wardrobe.

A MAN'S WARDROBE

And now, for men, here is a simple list.

> 5-7 T-shirts or dress shirts in different colors
> 5-7 jackets in different styles and colors
> 6 pairs of slacks/ pants in different types and colors
> 2 pairs of jeans
> 4 pairs of shoes: runners, comfy pair, office dress, casual or work boots
> 1 suit
> 1 tuxedo
> 5-7 ties

This amount will give a gentleman 60 different looks, enough for two months without wearing the same thing twice.

Daily Prayer

Dear God, I pray for a heart of gratitude as I witness the positive changes in my home and closet. Please help me appreciate the transformation and find joy in my life's newfound order and simplicity. Help me to arrange my wardrobe to be simple and pleasing to you. Thank you, Lord. In Jesus' name, I pray, Amen.

Questions

"What do I have in my wardrobe that I despise?"

"Am I going to give it away or throw it away?"

Write your answer below before you go on to day 11.

Affirmation

"I embrace a minimalist mindset and create a wardrobe that reflects my true style and brings me joy."

DAY 11

DECLUTTERING AND ORGANIZING KITCHEN SPACES

Mark Twain once said, "The secret of getting ahead is getting started."

Today's Bible Verse

"But everything should be done in a fitting and orderly way."
1 Corinthians 14:40

In some homes, the kitchen is the hub of all the activity. Everyone congregates around the table or island where mom talks, cooks, or drinks tea or coffee. Most homes are set up like the lady of the house wants it to be.

I remember watching the movie, "Julie & Julia", with Amy Adams as the blogger and Meryl Streep as Julia Child. The movie was about Julie, a blogger who just loved Julia Child and decided to write a blog about her experiences every night after cooking one of Julia Child's recipes from her famous book "French Cooking" by Julia Child. The movie flashed from blogger Julie's kitchen to Julia Child's kitchen, showing how it was going as she made each recipe.

Julia Child's kitchen was immaculate, a place for everything and everything in its place, while our blogger Julie's kitchen was small, crowded, and rather messy. What is your kitchen like? Is everything in its place, or is it a bit messy?

After my mother passed away, I had the privilege of cleaning her house and preparing it for sale. I had moved away a few years before her passing, so I didn't realize until I cleaned her kitchen out that she had a whole extra cupboard full of different little kitchen gadgets to help in her culinary skills, such as a hot dog zapper cooker, a Starfrit apple peeler, a vegetable slicer, a jar opener, a salad spinner, a jelly mold, and many other interesting items. You can get sucked in. Today, I bought an electric potato/apple peeler that will save my arthritic hands from a lot of pain.

Many were used once or twice, then put away for safekeeping until that rainy day came along when she would drag it out again. Manufacturers develop new gadgets that will make our kitchens more efficient yearly. It is often just more stuff to clutter up our counter or cupboard spaces.

Organize your kitchen by grouping smaller items together and creating designated storage spaces, such as a baking shelf and drawer, a cooking shelf and drawer, pots and pans, storage containers, cutlery, etc. Organize your kitchen cabinets and drawers and discard any duplicates or unused items. Keep your eye on how many storage containers you keep. These often get out of hand.

Organization takes you from a chaotic kitchen to a more efficient kitchen. Use what you have, and don't let it clutter your space. Put appliances away when you are not using them. More isn't always the best.

Daily Prayer

Heavenly Father, I seek Your guidance and wisdom as I decide what to keep and let go of in my kitchen. You know what I will need and what I won't. Please help me keep what I need and give the rest away. Fill me with joy and peace as I create a space that aligns with Your plan for my kitchen life. Thank you, Father. In Jesus' name, I pray, Amen.

Questions

"What area in my kitchen am I having a space problem with?"

_____

_____

_____

_____

_____

"What things in my kitchen do not have a home?" Now, please write down your answer below, what you will do to declutter enough space to make room for them in your kitchen. Finish this task before you start day 12.

_____

_____

_____

_____

_____

Affirmation

"I create an orderly and functional kitchen, making meal preparation a joyful and efficient experience."

Notes, Ideas, Thoughts & Prayers

DAY 12

EMBRACING MINIMALISM IN THE KITCHEN

Someone once said, "Happiness is not found in the abundance of possessions but in the simplicity of the heart." – Unknown

Today's Bible Verse

The story of Mary and Martha. Luke 10:38-42

38 As Jesus and his disciples were on their way, he came to a village where a woman named Martha opened her home to him. 39 She had a sister called Mary, who sat at the Lord's feet listening to what he said.

40 But Martha was distracted by all the preparations that had to be made. She came to him and asked, "Lord, don't you care that my sister has left me to do the work by myself? Tell her to help me!"

41 "Martha, Martha," the Lord answered, "you are worried and upset about many things, 42 but few things are needed—or indeed only one. [a] Mary has chosen what is better, and it will not be taken away from her."

Mary and Martha were sisters. Jesus and his disciples decided to come over for lunch after ministering and sharing with the people outside. They were friends, so this was a normal thing. On this day, Mary was excited to come and listen to what Jesus had to say, so she came into the house and sat down with him to listen to his teaching. Mary wanted to sit at Jesus' feet, relax and listen.

On the other hand, Martha was thinking of the task at hand, preparing a meal for these hungry men. As the afternoon wore on and Martha was still slaving in the kitchen, Mary took no notice and continued to sit at Jesus's feet, listening to his every word. Finally, exasperated Martha stormed into the room. She complained to Jesus that Mary wasn't pulling her weight by helping with the meal and preparations. Jesus' reply was true and not fair in Martha's eyes.

Are you a Mary or a Martha? _____

Do you take the time to smell the flowers, to sit at the feet of Jesus, or are you so busy making meals, missing out on what is around you and the people who need your listening ear? _____

_____

_____

_____

Why not simplify your kitchen by donating or selling unused appliances, utensils, or gadgets you rarely use to those in need? Do you need more than one ice cream scoop or measuring cup? Get organized and give away any duplicate items to a young mother just starting out or to those in need.

Daily Prayer

Father God, I pray for a joyful and hopeful mindset throughout this decluttering journey. Help me to focus on the possibilities and the blessings that await me as I create a more organized and peaceful kitchen and home. In Jesus' name, I pray, Amen.

Questions

"What area in my kitchen am I having a space problem with?"

"What items in my kitchen do I never use?" Write them down before you look at day 13.

Affirmation

"I let go of excess in my kitchen, keeping only the items I truly need, love, and use."

Notes, Ideas, Thoughts & Prayers

DAY 13

DECLUTTERING AND ORGANIZING LIVING SPACES

Deepak Chopra once said, "In the midst of movement and chaos, keep stillness inside of you."

Today's Bible Verse

"Be still and know that I am God; I will be exalted among the nations, I will be exalted in the earth." Psalm 46:10

Jane's home: Many years ago, I visited this very rich lady in the Bayview area of Toronto. I was excited to visit her as I hadn't visited a rich person before. I drove up her driveway and remembered thinking, what a beautiful home, such a lovely, manicured lawn. I knocked on the door, and Jane opened the door to let me in. I followed her into her kitchen and was shocked at how much stuff she had everywhere. She had so much stuff that there was no place to sit down.

Jane was a hoarder. At that point in time, this was my first experience with one. Every kitchen drawer was open and full, and the counter was full. Every chair was full of books and magazines, with newspapers and flyers all over the tables. I was shocked that anyone could let their stuff get so out of control. I could feel the stress just walking into her home. I left there feeling so sad. What a beautiful, expensive home that was a waste as she couldn't live in it and enjoy what God had given her.

I remember moving back into my mom and dad's home as an adult for a short season of my life and being there when they moved to a new home. My dad was a bit of a hoarder behind the scenes, not like Jane, where there was no place to sit but a hoarder in hiding.

I remember Dad collecting the daily newspaper because he wanted to keep the crossword puzzle and another puzzle in them every night. So, instead of cutting the two puzzles out of the daily newspaper and putting them in a box, he kept the whole newspaper and stored them in the attic.

He would say that when he retired, he could look back and see what happened on a specific date in time. They didn't have Google or the Internet in those days. Dad loved the information and didn't want to be unable to read about events from his past in the future.

Moving day came, and Dad's stuff was still not packed up. He had so many newspapers in the attic that mom wouldn't let him take them to the new house. He was devastated but eventually got over it. At one point, I suggested that Dad throw them out the window to the lower deck of the house, so they didn't have to carry them down the stairs. Mom wouldn't have it. What would the neighbors think? So, he left them there.

Did you know that taking just 10 minutes a day will de-stress you and relax you for your whole day? We need to learn how to be still and soak in the Lord. We must designate a space in our home to relax and connect with God and our inner self.

We need to declutter a space in our living area or bedroom that is peaceful and pleasing to our eyes and inner being. Arrange aesthetically pleasing items so we can walk into that room and feel and be at peace.

Daily Prayer

Dear God, I ask for Your strength to resist the temptation to accumulate unnecessary belongings. Help me find joy in the freedom of a clutter-free life and the ability to bless others with my abundance. Help my heart not to be too upset when I let go of things. Thank you Lord. In Jesus' name, I pray. Amen.

Questions

"What is in my living and family rooms that I struggle to let go of?"

"Why do you think that you are struggling with it?"

Now, ask God to help you let it go. Write down your struggle below before going to day 14.

Affirmation

"I create a serene and inviting living room where my family and I can relax and connect."

Notes, Ideas, Thoughts & Prayers

DAY 14

CREATING A COZY AND CLUTTER-FREE LIVING ROOM

Someone once said, "A cluttered room is a cluttered mind. An organized room is an organized mind." Unknown

Today's Bible Verse

"For God is not a God of disorder but of peace—as in all the congregations of the Lord's people." 1 Corinthians 14:33

My mother was a clean freak. Everything had to be put in its place most of the time. After we used something, it had to be put back in its place. My dear mom always told us to shut the door, not let the flies in, hang up your coats, take off your shoes, etc., and we did. Our home was always so clean, and people commented on how neat and tidy it was.

Every night after my dad read the daily newspaper, it had to be folded back just as before he read it and put in the magazine rack. He wasn't allowed to keep it on the coffee table. No, it had to be put back in the magazine rack perfectly folded. I suspect that was from my mother's upbringing in poverty and the fear of the possibility of the Children's Aid coming and taking my brother and me away because she wasn't a fit mother. She was a good mother, and we all knew it.

You could sit in Mom's living room any time of the day or night and feel calm, relaxed, and at peace because it was always tidy and clean, everything in its place.

Having a clean living room meant guests could pop in anytime without worrying about ever being embarrassed that your home was not tidy. Mess and physical clutter does stress your mind whether you think it does or not, so declutter and have a peaceful place to relax.

To do this, you must practice a daily decluttering habit, such as putting things back in their designated spots after you use them and before you go to bed.

Create a cozy corner in the living room by decluttering unnecessary items and adding soft furnishings and personal touches. You will love yourself for doing that for sure.

Daily Prayer

Father, please help me to have a joyful and positive attitude as I tackle each decluttering task in my living room and family room. Let my enthusiasm inspire others in my family to want to clean up after themselves as well so we can create an atmosphere of encouragement and joy. Thank you, Lord. In Jesus' name, I pray, Amen.

Questions

"What must I do to make my living room and family room more warm, cozy, and friendly?" Write your thoughts below before you start day 15.

_____

_____

_____

_____

Affirmation

"I create a clutter-free environment that supports my well-being and brings peace to my mind and spirit."

Notes, Ideas, Thoughts & Prayers

DAY 15

DECLUTTERING DIGITAL SPACE MANAGING TECHNOLOGY

Someone once said, "Clear your digital clutter to create space for meaningful connections.' Unknown

Today's Bible Verse

"God is our refuge and strength, an ever-present help in trouble." Psalm 46:1

After both my parents died, my brother David bought an expensive computer with his inheritance money. He filled it so full of programs that he could no longer use it as it was too full, and the programs didn't have enough room to run.

I remember starting on Windows 3, which was so simple to use I knew it inside and out. Then came Windows 4, 5, 7, 10, and now Windows 11. Every year, they come out with another level with more to learn that is much more complicated. Reviewing your files and deleting old ones you no longer need is important.

When did you last review your document, download, or e-mail files? Do you remember?

Instead of buying more space to put more documents and pictures in, go through them and delete the duplicate files and those that you no longer need. If you do this, your computer will run more efficiently and quickly. You will be happy you did.

Will we ever read everything we have kept on our computers? Take time to learn how to downsize your information, your emails, and your downloads on your computer.

Clutter on our computers takes up space, bogging down your computer efficiency. Organize and declutter your digital files and e-mails, deleting unnecessary ones and creating folders for easy access to the ones you keep.

Dedicate time to decluttering your digital spaces, such as your e-mail inbox or computer desktop, and organize each file and folder. Keep only what you need. Too much information will blow your system and blow your mind. You can purchase outer storage places to keep your old files.

Daily Prayer

Lord, as I organize my possessions and my computer files. I pray for the ability to prioritize what I truly need to keep. Please help guide me to make intentional choices as I go through my technical stuff. Show me what I need to keep and what I need to delete. Thank you, Lord. In Jesus' name, I pray, Amen.

Questions

"What do I need to declutter from my digital files on my computer, e-mail, and phone?" Set a date to work on this in your journal before you begin Day 16.

Affirmation

"I declutter my digital spaces, organizing my digital life and creating a sense of clarity and focus."

DAY 16

TACKLING PAPER CLUTTER MANAGING DOCUMENTS AND MAIL

Seneca once said, "The greatest wealth is a poverty of desires."

Today's Bible Verse

> "Live in harmony with one another. Do not be proud but be willing to associate with people of low positions. Do not be conceited." Romans 12:16

My Mom hated mess, and Dad was 'a messy'. She hated how my dad kept his office so messy and how he always waited 90 days to pay bills. She was always looking for ways to keep his desk tidy.

Dad just hated anyone touching his desk and mixing up his piles of papers and stuff. How would she clean up his office and desk without him getting mad at her? She thought about it and came up with the most brilliant idea. "I know; I'll ask Jo to do it. Give it to Jo to do, and he won't be able to get mad at her." And that is what she did.

If you wait 90 days to pay your bills, watch what happens. Phone calls, e-mails, letters from the bill collectors wanting their money and their bills paid, then the interest does add up if you haven't paid them.

For me, this is unacceptable; for my dad, it was the norm. He said, "They aren't using my money to make interest off me!"

I pay my bills as soon as they come in the mail, before the due date, so they are always paid on time. I get so upset when I have to pay a penny in interest. When you have a messy desk, you can't find the bills to pay and must clean it up to find them. If you declutter, this won't happen to you, and you'll never have to pay interest due to paying your bills late.

Try touching each piece of paper only once. Pay your bills on time and pay no interest. Set up a designated area for sorting and managing incoming mail and papers, such as a mail organizer or filing system for paying bills. Why not reflect on Matthew 6:19-21 and declutter your home to store treasures in heaven?

Daily Prayer

Father, I pray for joy and fulfillment as I simplify my surroundings. Let me find delight in the beauty and functionality of an organized home, knowing that it reflects Your order and creativity. Please help me to implement what I have learned to put my business affairs in order, like paying my bills on time and knowing where all my important papers are. Thank you Father. In Jesus' name, Amen

Questions

"What must I do to lessen or eliminate my paper clutter?"

"What must I do to make my space neat and tidy?" Write this in your journal before you go on to day 17.

Affirmation

"I release attachments to material possessions and find contentment in the simplicity and beauty of my surroundings."

DAY 17

ORGANIZING AND SIMPLIFYING YOUR HOME OFFICE OR WORKSPACE

Someone once said, "An organized space promotes an organized mind." Unknown

And that is so needed in an office workspace. Would you not agree?

Today's Bible Verse

> *"Then make my joy complete by being like-minded, having the same love, being one in spirit and of one mind." Philippians 2:2*

Since Covid, I have worked from home. I love my office as it is organized and very efficient. It takes up two walls in an L-shape in a corner of my bedroom. When it gets cluttered, I cannot work. Being organized helps me not to get distracted when I have much to get done in a day. I have learned to be organized out of necessity.

Some people work with piles of paper, like my dad. He had piles all over his desk, which looked like organized chaos. Dad swore by his system, and I swore by mine. I like to work with files to see what I have and find it easily. With piles, you must go through each piece of paper when looking for something to find what you want. Files are more organized; you can have them alphabetically for easy access. (In my opinion, of course)

I also use narrow paper trays to organize all the types of work. I can see what needs to be done immediately as I look at my labeled paper trays. When a paper tray is full, I take it, process the papers in it, and then go on to the next paper tray.

I have used this method for the past 17 years, and it works well for me. This way, I only touch the paper twice, first when I put it in its designated paper tray and second when I process it for good.

Here is the plan I have used for many years. It may work for you.

3 Main Boxes:	IN PENDING OUT
Main Files:	Mail, To do, To read, To sign, To pay, To file
Subject Files:	that pertain to your work specifically.
Month Files:	Jan, Feb, March to Dec (File sheets 1 to 31)
Weekly Files:	Mon Tues, Wed, Thurs, Fri, Sat, Sun

You can get more work done in an organized space. When it is cluttered, you spend half your time looking for the paper you need to work on.

Set up an organized and inspiring workspace by decluttering unnecessary papers, organizing office supplies, and creating a designated work area.

Establish an efficient and organized workspace by decluttering your desk, organizing your supplies, and implementing a filing system.

Daily Prayer

Heavenly Father, help me to organize my office so I can be more efficient when doing my work, finances, and dealing with my mail and other paperwork. I surrender this area to you and thank you for helping me do this your way. In Jesus' name, I pray, Amen.

Questions

"What must I do to declutter and make my Home office more efficient?"

Think about it, make a plan, and write it down below. Complete this task before you go on to day 18.

Affirmation

"I establish an organized and inspiring workspace that fuels my productivity and creativity."

Notes, Ideas, Thoughts & Prayers

DAY 18

DECLUTTERING AND STREAMLINING YOUR CLEANING ROUTINE

Pearl Buck once said, "Order is the shape upon which beauty depends."

Today's Bible Verse

"The Lord makes firm the steps of the one who delights in him." Psalm 37:23

We learn from those around us. I learned a lot from my mom. She had a household routine that worked well for her and has worked well for me. You, too, can create a routine for yourself like she did to keep your home clean all the time.

With Mom's routine, there were no worries when someone popped in with no notice, as her place was clean and tidy 99% of the time with her weekly routine.

- Monday was the bathroom and wash day for all our soiled clothes.
- Tuesday, she did the ironing, something many don't do today.
- Wednesday was always her scrumptious baking day.
- Thursday became her cleaning, vacuuming, and polishing day. Polishing makes everything sparkle, etc.
- Friday was always the washing and waxing of the floors.

- Saturday became shopping, gardening, changing beds, shoe shining (Dad's job), bath night, etc.
- Sunday was Church, lunch, nap time, church, and bedtime.

We repeat the routine every week forever and ever, amen. If you can't do your routine one day here and one day there, it is no big deal, as the routine will keep your home in good shape. Just continue to stick to a routine, and you will be fine.

Many say that 'Cleanliness is next to Godliness', perhaps not, but it does help.

Making a cleaning routine for your life will keep you consistent and keep you on track in keeping your home organized and tidy. Your routine will also keep you stress-free.

Why not find three items in your home that you can repurpose or rearrange to create a more harmonious environment this week? Research and adopt a simple and effective cleaning routine that works for you and suits your lifestyle and preferences.

Daily Prayer

Dear God, help me to approach decluttering with a spirit of celebration rather than a sense of burden. Please help me to create a routine that will work well for me and get what I want done. In Jesus' name, Amen.

Questions

"What do I need to do to put it in place to keep my house clean?"

Make a plan, a routine, and write it down before you start day 19.

Affirmation

"I bring order and harmony to my surroundings, creating a peaceful atmosphere in my home."

DAY 19

DECLUTTERING AND ORGANIZING CHILDREN'S SPACES

Coco Chanel once said, "Simplicity is the keynote of all true elegance."

Today's Bible Verse

"Start children off on the way they should go, and even when they are old, they will not turn from it." Proverbs 22:6

When I was 8 years old, I had an older friend, Joanne, who had this amazing playroom. It was upstairs in her home and was so bright, with wrap-around windows on three sides of the room. It was so organized, with a place for everything and everything in its place.

She had a play area for many activities, such as painting, drawing, reading, dolls and clothes, balls, chalkboards, board games, etc. It was the perfect room for children to play in for hours and hours.

Several years later, we moved, and I met a new friend, Jody, who also had a cool playroom. Her playroom was in her basement in her recreation room. Her play area was split into two areas; one was like a school room with desks, a chalkboard, and a teacher's desk.

The other area was set up like a store, with shelves with products and shopping carts that we could take and go around the room and pick out products we could buy with our fake money. I remember how much fun it was to go around the room and put my fake things in my cart to buy with fake money at the cashier. What a brilliant setup to teach children the value of money and things.

My brother and I had a playroom in the basement. It was a big recreation area where we could play floor hockey, dance, have a tea party, or lounge around. Under the two sets of steps, my brother and I each had our own little storage areas where we kept all our stuff, our treasures.

It was big enough to put a small bookcase in and a pillow and blanket. We would go into our own little area and read for hours, Dave in his corner and I in mine.

Every family is different and will set up a play area to cater to their own family's needs. Organization will help your child learn, grow, and develop, no matter how big or small the room is. Teaching your children, the importance of keeping things neat and tidy and cleaning up after themselves is important.

Teaching your children, the importance of decluttering their own spaces is valuable. This will teach them the gift of letting go of their toys as they outgrow them and give them to other children who can't afford them. It is important to make decluttering a game and cleaning up fun. This will help your children grow in their ability to care for their environment and love others. Teach them to think outside of themselves to those in need. This will help make them more compassionate people.

Daily Prayer

Lord, help me to teach my kids the value of their things, to take care of them, to share them with others, and to let go of them for good and not hold on to them forever. Help us all to hold onto things lightly. In Jesus' name, I pray. Amen.

Questions

"What is in my kids' playroom or bedroom that I need to declutter the most?" Write down your answer before you go on to day 20.

_____

_____

_____

_____

_____

_____

_____

Affirmation

"I teach my children the value of decluttering and fostering a sense of gratitude and appreciation for their belongings."

DAY 20

TEACHING CHILDREN THE VALUE OF SIMPLICITY

Dr. A. Witham once said, "Children spell love... T_I_M_E."

Today's Bible Verse

"Therefore everyone who hears these words of mine and puts them into practice is like a wise man who built his house on the rock." Matthew 7:24

A child's character is developed and solid in the first 5 years of life. After that, they still learn but can't change their basic character. Teaching them while they are young will set them up for success.

Spend time with your kids; they are watching you. Quality of time, not necessarily quantity, goes much farther in building their characters.

When you are with your kids, be present with them, not just in the room, paying attention to them and letting them know you are listening.

Look them in the eye at their eye level, and what you say to them will be acknowledged more than if you don't.

Teach them the importance of people, love and forgive, share and give, and think outwardly, selfless rather than selfish.

Teach your children while they are young, spend quality time with them, and show them the value of simplicity. Teach them the value of love, forgiveness, and generosity and that people are more important than stuff.

Cultivate a spirit of generosity in your child by decluttering and donating toys, clothes, or books to those in need.

Teach your children the importance of gratitude and giving by encouraging them to have a big heart to share with others.

Daily Prayer

Dear God, I pray for patience and perseverance as I navigate the ups and downs of decluttering. Please help me to make it fun for the sake of my children. Teach them that people are more important than stuff and that giving is more important than receiving. Fill them with Your joy and show them the gift of blessing that comes from letting go. In Jesus' name. I pray, Amen

Questions

"How do I teach my children to live simply when I am just learning this myself?"

_____

_____

_____

_____

_____

"How do I teach my children to pick up after themselves, to hang up their clothes and put away their toys?" Show me, Lord. Write your thoughts below before you begin day 21.

Affirmation

"I instill in my children the joy of giving and sharing as we declutter and donate items to those in need."

DAY 21

DECLUTTERING AND ORGANIZING MY BATHROOM AND TOILETRIES

Today's Bible Verse

> *"Peace I leave with you; my peace I give you. I do not give to you as the world gives. Do not let your hearts be troubled, and do not be afraid." John 14:27*

Overstocking items may seem great to save some money but take it from me. In the long run, it isn't. You never use everything all the time. You might throw out much of what you bought as the chemicals in the products change the longer you keep them.

A bargain isn't always a bargain, especially if we can't use the item before the expiry date.

Why not create a calming bathroom environment by decluttering and organizing your bathroom cabinets and drawers and discarding expired or unused toiletries?

Expiry dates are so important to pay attention to. Declutter with these dates in mind. They say that makeup needs to be disposed of every three months. I know it is expensive, but when you use old makeup, it is soiled and starts changing its chemical structure, and it can be dangerous if you are using old makeup.

When I was a teenager, a lady from a famous makeup brand came to my house to do a makeover for me. I looked so beautiful for a day until I woke up the next morning. For a week after the makeover, I broke out into a terrible, embarrassing rash on my face due to the expired makeup. How old is your makeup?

A few years later, as a young pastor, I went to a denominational retreat with a bad cold. I took some cold medication to try to mask the symptoms, but instead of helping, I got worse and started to hallucinate. No, I wasn't on illicit drugs, as they thought.

The nurse called and asked me what I was taking. I gave her my package, and she noticed the cold medication had expired. I never even thought to look at the expiry date. She explained that the chemicals change their components as they age and that I should never use expired medication. I spent the night in the infirmary, where the nurse could watch over me in case, I got any worse.

A few years ago, I was listening to the news on the radio where the announcer was talking about a cake mix that killed a young girl. This was shocking, so I listened intently to discover that the girl had used a cake mix that had expired two years before. She got food poisoning and died when she made and ate the cake.

I always check expiry dates on boxed and dry goods to make sure they are still safe to use. The reason she died was that the chemicals in the cake mix had changed their structure.

It is scary, and these things could all have been avoided if we all had checked the expiry dates. Has any of your medication expired? Check the expiry dates on your makeup, medication, and food, especially dry goods. It will save you and your family a lot of trouble. Expiry dates are there for a reason.

Daily Prayer

Heavenly Father, Thank You for the joy of sharing my excess with those in need. Guide me to donate and bless others with a generous and joyful heart. Please help me not buy impulsively to save money but to ask you for your wisdom at the time. Please protect me and my family from the chemical changes in anything that we consume. Thank you, Father. In Jesus' name, I pray, Amen.

Questions

"What is in your medicine cabinet or bathroom cupboard causing chaos and mess that you need to eliminate?" Please write it down here and how you feel about it and get rid of it before you go on to day 22.

_____

_____

_____

_____

_____

_____

_____

Affirmation

"I transform my bathroom into a tranquil oasis, free from clutter and filled with serenity."

Notes, Ideas, Thoughts & Prayers

DAY 22

CREATING A RESTFUL AND DECLUTTERED BEDROOM

Someone once said, "A restful mind is a decluttered mind." – unknown.

Today's Bible Verse

"In their hearts humans plan their course, but the Lord establishes their steps." Proverbs 16:9

I first recall my brother Dave's bedroom when he was 10 to 13. It was a war zone, always in turmoil, with stuff on the floor, bed never made, and things everywhere. When he got older as a teenager, his bedroom changed. First, he moved to the basement, where he had the whole recreation room with a bathroom.

It was a small apartment that my grandmother used to live in. When she moved out, Dave moved in. The difference was that he liked it and thought it was cool, so he took pride in his space and kept it clean for the most part. He turned it into a man cave, which was fun, relaxing, and cool. His friends loved it as they now had a place to hang out.

Make your bed every day. It is the first accomplishment of the day and sets you and your day up for success. It will set your mind at ease and bring peace and motivation to your day.

Set out clothes hampers so you don't have to throw your clothes on the floor, where you must pick them up later, setting yourself up to succeed again. Each step leads to a decluttered room and a decluttered mindset that will help you sleep well, too.

Create a clutter-free bedroom by decluttering items that do not contribute to a peaceful sleep environment. Declutter surfaces, organize your clothing, and simplify your décor. Remove all your electronics from your bedroom or turn them off for a more peaceful sleep.

Daily Prayer

Lord, I pray for a spirit of gratitude as I witness the positive impact of decluttering and organizing my bedroom and life. Let my heart overflow with joy for the blessings of creating an intentional and peaceful space. In Jesus' name, I pray, Amen.

Questions

"What area do I need to improve in my bedroom?" Write it down in your journal and do it before day 23.

_____
_____
_____
_____
_____
_____
_____
_____

Affirmation

"I create a peaceful and clutter-free bedroom where I can rest and rejuvenate each night."

Notes, Ideas, Thoughts & Prayers

DAY 23

DECLUTTERING AND ORGANIZING THE GARAGE AND STORAGE AREAS

Albert Einstein once shared, "Out of clutter, find simplicity."

Today's Bible Verse

"Search me, God, and know my heart; test me and know my anxious thoughts. See if there is any offensive way in me and lead me in the way everlasting." Psalm 139:23- 24

Create organized areas in your garage, basement, or storage areas for tools, seasonal stuff, extra stuff, etc. Use appropriate containers for inside and outside; when you go to get what you need, you won't have a problem.

It is important to find the right containers for storage space. When storing things in your garage, you need containers with a good seal so the mice and other critters can't get in.

Last summer, a friend wanted to use my sewing machine, which I had stored on a shelf in the garage. I said, "Sure," and went to get it. To my shock, when I found it, it was covered with mouse pee and poop. I had to clean and sterilize it before loaning it to her. The mice had set up residence in my garage and made a mess of much of my stuff, as my things were not in sealed containers but in boxes or just lying on the shelves.

A few years back, I had a couple stay in my home for about a month, and while they were there, the wife decided to make some cookies. She took my flour out of the cupboard and found weevils (bugs) throughout my bag of flour. I don't use flour much, so I didn't notice the infestation. Coming home from work and finding bugs in my pantry was embarrassing. For inside organization, putting foodstuff in airtight containers and checking the expiry dates is important.

Tupperware is the best-sealed container on the market. Missionary friends swear it is the only container they use overseas to keep the bugs out. They have used other cheaper brands, and the little critters could get in and spoil their food and grains.

Remember to sort and declutter items in your garage and storage spaces by donating or discarding what you don't need to bless others.

Daily Prayer

Dear God, I ask You for the strength to resist the temptation to compare my progress with others. Please fill me with joy and contentment as I focus on my own journey and celebrate each step forward. Thank you for giving me your grace in this process. In Jesus' name, I pray. Amen.

Questions

"What's taking up too much space in my garage or storage area?"

Please write it down below and make a plan for how to declutter your garage. Finish this before you start day 24.

Affirmation

"I declutter and organize my garage and storage spaces, creating order and reclaiming valuable space."

Notes, Ideas, Thoughts & Prayers

DAY 24

SIMPLIFYING HOME DÉCOR FINDING BEAUTY IN SIMPLICITY

My creative decorator made my house a home on a shoestring budget. You can, too!

Today's Bible Verse

"Love does no harm to a neighbor. Therefore, love is the fulfillment of the law." Romans 13:10

My friend Shirley had an eye for simplicity and beauty with the ability to make beauty out of a few small things. I remember going to a craft store with her one day to find items to make a wreath for our living room wall above the couch.

I was amazed at how she could take a bit of straw, a bird, a flower or two, and some greenery to create this beautiful coral wreath. The color and beauty made the room pop. It was just what the bare wall needed. She had the eye and made our house a home with her little touches in every room.

Little things make a wonderful difference and add to a room. I remember making seat cushions, placemats, and a table runner for our eating area in one country home we lived in. It just set the room off with a warm and cozy feeling where everyone wanted to sit at the table with a cup of tea.

Plants add more than décor, giving off oxygen during the day. Ferns in the bathroom bring a natural splash of beauty and thrive in the damp environment.

Everyone has an idea of what their home should look like. Some are too sparse with no décor, others are too crowded with a mishmash of stuff, and still others, with a gift of decorating, make their house into a beautiful home. If you don't have that gift, why not ask the Lord what you need in a given space or area?

If you have a friend with that gift, why not ask for their opinion or help? You can also hire an interior decorator if you are desperate. if you need it and ask others with the gift of decorating to help as well.

You can pick up some great ideas from home and garden magazines in print and online. Make notes of your ideas in your journal and put them in place when you have the means and time to do so. It will give your home that look of elegance and warmth.

More stuff won't give you a more elegant look. Less can be more and warmer in many cases. One or two items on a table can be more elegant than many misplaced pieces. Experiment, and ask your friends for their comments and advice. Some people have an eye for décor.

Embrace minimalism by decluttering decorative items and creating a clean, simple, aesthetic look, in your home. Practice simplicity in your home décor by selecting a few meaningful and aesthetically pleasing items to display while keeping your surfaces clear and uncluttered.

Daily Prayer

Father, I pray for a joyful and lighthearted approach to organizing. Please help me find the right items that will bring warmth into each room. Help me to find laughter and delight in the process, knowing that a joyful heart is a key ingredient for success. In Jesus' name, Amen.

Questions

"What home decorating style do you love in your home?"

"What room do you want to start to decorate first or redecorate and why?"

Write down your thoughts below before you begin day 25.

Affirmation

"I cultivate simplicity and elegance in my home, letting go of excess and embracing a minimalist aesthetic."

Notes, Ideas, Thoughts & Prayers

DAY 25

LETTING GO OF CLUTTERED RELATIONSHIPS AND BOUNDARIES

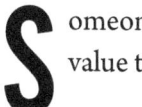

Someone once said, "Surround yourself with people who add value to your life." Unknown.

Today's Bible Verse

"And whatever you do, in word or deed, do it all in the name of the Lord Jesus, giving thanks to God the Father through him." Colossians 3:17

Now that you are decluttering the junk in your home, have you ever thought about your relationships that need to be decluttered? Why not take stock and make a list of all the people in your life who bring you down, who are negative around you, and those who always insult or demean you?

Make a list in your journal and start to pray for them.

Do you have any "Klingons", those who zap your energy anytime they are around you or constantly waste your time? Or people who try to control you? We all have them, but how do we change it so we don't spend as much time with them?

One lady calls me several times a day to ask questions or complain. Usually, I can get her off the phone, but sometimes I can't, and it gets very frustrating because she is wasting my time. Another lady who calls is always in a crisis. To her, it is a crisis. To me, not so much. She needs someone to talk her through what she is going through.

And I have had many others through the years who have taken up my time energy and tried to be in control of our relationships.

How did I, and how do I handle them when they come into my life? I have had to declutter my relationships by setting boundaries and not being afraid to say no. We will talk further about learning to say no on Day 26.

I have had to set boundaries by not answering phone calls from these dear ones during my off hours and weekends and waiting until Monday to call them back. I have had to set time limits on my calls, where I set the time limit, not them.

I have arranged a support system for some, and I insist that I am unavailable now and that they need to contact their support person, not me. I told them I would call them back next week and mark it on my calendar, so I don't forget. I put their name and number in my phone so when they do call me. I can see who is calling before I decide whether to take their call or not. They can always leave a message, and if it is urgent, you can call them back.

I try to focus on positive relationships and eliminate negative relationships. I limit my time to those without boundaries, whom the enemy has sent to distract or waste my time. It has helped me live a happier, less frustrating life. I try to hang out with those who can give me life, not those who bring death, depression, and negativity to me.

- Focus on positive people who will bless you and not take from you.
- Spend time with those you can grow with, not those who hurt you.
- Evaluate your relationships and declutter toxic and negative influences from your life.
- Set boundaries with the people who bring unnecessary clutter or negativity into your life.

You will live longer and be so glad that you did.

Daily Prayer

Father God, I surrender my relationships to you. Will you show me who is toxic in my life, who is always negative, and who brings me down? Will you show me who you want me to hang out with and keep as my good friends, who bring only positive influence and joy into my life? I give You, my feelings. Only You can help me sort this all out in my life. Please fill me with joy and confidence in you. Thank you, Lord. In Jesus' name, I pray. Amen.

Questions

"What negative relationships do I need to let go of?"

"What toxic relationship am I in that I need to say no to and change?"

"What positive, encouraging relationships can I start?" Write them down below and start to pray for those people, asking God to make a way to help you let them go. Ask God to help you to pursue good friendships and let go of the bad ones. Do this before you start day 26.

Affirmation

"I surround myself with positive and uplifting relationships that contribute to a clutter-free and harmonious life."

DAY 26

DECLUTTERING YOUR TIME PRIORITIZING AND SAYING NO

Someone once said, "Don't be busy, be productive." Unknown.

Today's Bible Verse

"The fruit of righteousness will be peace; its effect will be quietness and confidence forever." Isaiah 32:17

Did you know that two-year-old children love to say "NO" even though they often don't mean it? They are learning to individuate, to express themselves, and to have a mind of their own. Haven't you heard that two-year-olds are the hardest to raise as they are labeled the terrible two-zees when they reach that age? That is why.

I remember listening to a recording of a famous singing couple in the 70's where the mother told a story about their son B. when he was just two years old. This famous family went to the ice cream parlor and asked Little B if he wanted an ice cream cone. He said, "No," then they asked him again, and he said, "No." They asked him a third time, and he still said, "No."

They then went into the ice cream parlor to buy ice cream cones for everyone but B. When B. realized that he did not get an ice cream, he started to cry. His dad quickly gave B. his and went back in and got another ice cream cone, realizing that B. meant yes even though he said "No."

It is time to evaluate your time. Who in your life are time wasters? Who takes your time and leaves you frustrated and feeling guilty? Say "No" to these time wasters. Say "No" to TV as it too can be a time waster in your life. Say "No" to social media or the internet if it is a time waster in your life.

If you have difficulty saying "NO", stand in front of a mirror, practice saying "NO!" and mean it. Ask God to give you the confidence and courage to share with those you need to say "No" to.

The more we say "No," the easier it is to say "No" and mean it. Some of us have difficulty saying "No" when we want to, as many people are too afraid to tell others how they feel. It is time to ask the Lord to help us to say "No" and mean it when we need to.

Start by decluttering your schedule by saying "No" to activities or commitments that do not line up with your values or priorities. Prioritize your time and commitments by learning to say "No" and re-aligning your values and goals.

Daily Prayer

Heavenly Father, I pray for discernment and wisdom as I decide what the time wasters in my life are. Help me say no to the people and things that will steal my time and help me seize the day. Please help me to make time for what is important and bring joy, purpose, and positive energy into my life. In Jesus' name, I pray. Amen.

Questions

"In what situation do I find it hard to say No?"

_____
_____
_____
_____
_____
_____

"In what circumstances do I find it hard to say "No?"

Write your thoughts below. Do this before you start day 27.

_____
_____
_____
_____
_____
_____

Affirmation

"I prioritize my time and commitments, saying "No" to activities that do not align with my values and goals."

Notes, Ideas, Thoughts & Prayers

DAY 27

THE BENEFITS OF DECLUTTERING FOR MENTAL AND EMOTIONAL WELL-BEING

Someone once said, "Declutter your mind, Simplify your life." Unknown

Today's Bible Verse

"In your relationships with one another, have the same mindset as Christ Jesus" Philippians 2:5

How can we declutter our minds and emotions today when we feel stressed?

David knew the answer to that he shared with us in Psalm 46:10, *"Be Still and know that I am God."* Being still, sitting at the feet of Jesus, and pouring your heart to Him.

To Soak, or not to Soak, that is the question.

When we look at the lives of Mary and Martha, from Luke 10:38-42, we see that Mary was the soaker and took the time to sit at the feet of Jesus. We also see that David soaked in the presence of his Father God, and God spoke to him. *"Be still and know that I am God."* Psalm 46:10

David was a great soaker and journaled about it all throughout his journal in the Psalms. Read everywhere David wrote his conversations down between him and God, his heavenly father.

Learn the Art of Soaking in the Lord and journaling, sharing your heart with God for your mental and emotional well-being. Learn how to pour your heart out before him and receive His peace in your heart. We must teach readers of the Word, the Art of soaking, and the Art of Journaling for their mental and emotional well-being. Learn how to unplug and soak in the Spirit of God for yourself.

Another way of putting it would be to learn how to practice mindfulness and declutter your mind by engaging in daily meditation or journaling, as King David did.

As you take this journey, reflect on the mental and emotional benefits of decluttering, noticing how a simplified environment positively affects your well-being. As you learn and practice these things, you will start to live in peace in your body, soul, and spirit, physically, mentally, and emotionally.

Daily Prayer

Dear God, please help me to make the time every day to soak in your presence and spend time with you. Teach me how to journal what you are showing me and telling me and how to rest in your love. Would you give me Your grace and guidance when I encounter challenges daily? Fill me with Your joy and remind me of the growth and transformation from spending time with you. In Jesus' name. Amen

Questions

"What am I still holding on to in my heart and mind that I am worried about or find it hard to let go of?"

_____

_____

_____

"What offenses am I still hanging on to?" Write it below and choose to forgive the people who offended you, choose to release them from your judgment, and choose to bless them.

Give them a gift they don't deserve, your forgiveness, and let it go. Let the offenses go and receive Father God's forgiveness and peace in your heart. Do this today before you begin day 28.

Affirmation

"I declutter not only my physical space but also my mind, releasing mental clutter, my heart, creating inner peace and my spirit, releasing His joy."

Notes, Ideas, Thoughts & Prayers

DAY 28

MAINTAINING A DECLUTTERED HOME HABITS AND SYSTEMS

Robert Collier once said, "Success is the sum of small efforts, repeated day in and day out.

Today's Bible Verse

"Therefore, my beloved brothers, be steadfast, immovable, always abounding in the work of the Lord, knowing that in the Lord your labor is not in vain." 1 Corinthians 15:58

The small changes we make each day make a big difference. Each small thing adds up to bigger changes in our environment. Consistency is the key. It takes 21 days to make a habit. 30 to make it stick. So, you go! Keep at it one day at a time, and you will see a big change in your life.

Be consistent like Daniel. Daniel lived a life of consistency. He prayed three times every day and thanked God for his goodness and blessing in his life. Even when praying to the true and living God became illegal, Daniel continued to pray to Him even when he knew it was against the law.

Yes, the law was changed, yet Daniel continued to pray to His God and ended up being thrown into a lion's den.

Daniel 6:10 When Daniel learned that the decree had been published, he went home to his upstairs room where the windows opened toward Jerusalem. Three times a day, he got down on his knees and prayed, giving thanks to his God, just as he had done before.

We can learn to keep going. Don't give up. You are on the brink of a miracle. *Galatians 6:9 says, 'Let us not become weary in doing good, for at the proper time we will reap a harvest if we do not give up.'*

Keep going and make decluttering a habit. It only takes about 15 minutes a day to make it happen, 15 minutes a day or 7.5 hours a month, or 90 hours a year, forever and ever, Amen.

Don't give up; be consistent like Daniel. Keep your daily habits and systems to maintain a decluttered home, such as tidying up before bed or dedicating 15 minutes a day to decluttering a particular room, area, closet, or drawer.

Celebrate your decluttering achievements by treating yourself to a special self-care activity you enjoy doing or rewarding yourself with something meaningful to you.

Daily Prayer

Father, I pray for a heart of gratitude for today. Please help me to find joy in the process of organizing. Please help me to be consistent, living one day at a time, continuing to do what you have called me to do. Thank you that this process is bringing blessings and great results into my life. In Jesus' name, Amen

Questions

"What new habits am I going to continue to keep making my home neat and tidy and declutter." Write them below before you start day 29.

Affirmation

"I celebrate my progress and accomplishments in decluttering, acknowledging the positive impact it has on my life."

DAY 29

CELEBRATING PROGRESS AND OVERCOMING DECLUTTERING CHALLENGES

Someone once said, "Progress, not perfection." – Unknown

Today's Bible Verse

"Casting all your anxieties on him, because he cares for you." 1 Peter 5:7

Take time to smell the flowers. Take time to breathe. Take time to celebrate the process and your progress, living one day at a time, enjoying life and the challenges that come along the way.

My mother's perfection was a stumbling block. Her home was immaculate, but she was always walking in fear, which made her a perfectionist. She never relaxed and was always afraid that Children's Aid would come and take us away because that happened when she was a child. She was a good mother and kept such a perfect home, so that would never have happened. If you have any fear or perfectionism, let it go.

Perfection is your enemy. Consistency is your friend. Just put one foot in front of the other and do what is expected each day. Follow your routine and watch what happens. Don't let anyone put anything on you. Be your own person, doing the best that you can with God's help.

Embrace the progress you have made and let go of your perfectionism. Celebrate your progress by acknowledging and appreciating how far you have come. You have already become a success in this process.

Daily Prayer

Lord, I thank You for the lessons learned through decluttering and organizing my home. Help me let go of perfectionism in every area of my life, especially when decluttering and organizing. Help me carry these lessons of simplicity, gratitude, and joy into my life. In Jesus' name, Amen.

Questions

"In what areas of my life am I a perfectionist?"

"What areas of my life need to be more consistent?"

Write your answer below before you go to day 30.

Affirmation

"I am already a success in this process!"

Notes, Ideas, Thoughts & Prayers

DAY 30

REFLECTING ON THE SPIRITUAL LESSONS LEARNED IN THIS DECLUTTERING JOURNEY

Someone once said, "Let your home be a haven of peace and a reflection of your heart."

Today's Bible Verse

"Honor the Lord with your wealth and with the first fruits of all your produce; then your barns will be filled with plenty, and your vats will be bursting with wine." Proverbs 3:9-10

How can we do that? Now that you have decluttered your house and made it into your peaceful home, invite the Holy Spirit and the Angelic host to stay and dwell there forever.

When you dedicate your space to the Lord, invite Him to have his way in your home every day. The Lord will bring his love, peace, and joy into your home. This will create the atmosphere of heaven in your home, where people feel His presence and won't want to leave. Welcome the Holy Spirit so there will be a tangible presence in each room.

Put on Christian inspirational or quiet worship music to play quietly in the background. This will bring the atmosphere of heaven into every room of your home.

We have cultivated the atmosphere of heaven in our home for several years and have had many angel encounters in each room. A few years ago, we had two ladies stay in our guest room upstairs. In the middle of the night, they both had an angel encounter in the night. When they got home the next day, one of their husbands called us to say that the power of the Lord had transformed his wife as a result of that powerful encounter.

A few years ago, my friend Shirley was dying of cancer at home, and we played soft music in a couple of the rooms. We couldn't figure out why the nurses would stay past their shifts before they went home each night.

We asked them, and several said it was so peaceful in our living room that they just loved to stay and sit there.

The presence of God and his angels were in that room, and they could feel it even though they couldn't express what they were feeling. It was a peaceful living room that no one wanted to leave. Many had powerful encounters with God there.

Cultivate the presence of the Lord in your home, too. If you do, He will come in His fullness with His presence, peace, and love for you. Create a daily, weekly, monthly, and yearly routine to maintain His presence as you declutter your home inside and out.

Dedicate a few moments each day to tidy up and stay organized. Enjoy your new home, and Praise God for this wonderful journey together. Congratulations! You made it! Keep up the good work!

Daily Prayer

Father God, I come to You with a heart of thanksgiving, thankful for all you have done to help me on this 30-day decluttering and organizing journey. Thank you for the wisdom and revelation You have shown me and the tips and tricks of organizing my life. Please help me to continue with this process to keep moving forward.

Holy Spirit, would you come and reign in my home? Would you send the host of heaven to come and minister to all who come into my home? You are welcome here every day, so come and fill this place with your love and life, your peace and joy. In Jesus' name, I pray. Amen.

Questions

"How am I going to keep a peaceful atmosphere in my home on an ongoing basis?" Ask God to help you.

Write your plan and a commitment prayer below. Do this as your commitment to the Lord and to keep your home neat and tidy.

Affirmation

"I create a sanctuary of love, peace, and order in my home, where I can rest and relax and recharge my body, soul, and spirit."

Notes, Ideas, Thoughts & Prayers

ACKNOWLEDGMENTS

I would like to acknowledge the following people for going beyond the call of duty in getting this book to print.

My Father God, Jesus, and Holy Spirit for their inspiration, insight, and gifts in enabling me to write and layout this book this way.

Donna Partow, and her team, who walked me through this process, sharing their expertise with me and our Book Launch group.

Brandon & Sandra Abrahams, Juanita Lubin, Lisa Ohata, Mary Audrey Raycroft, and Shelley Marques for their wonderful editing skills. Great Job, everyone, and thank you so much.

For my many intercessors who kept me in prayer through this process.

For my many family and friends who encouraged me along the way.

Here is a great big thank you to each and every one of you. I love you all so very much! Thank you for always being there for me.

I would like to thank you, my reader, for picking this book up to help you on your decluttering journey. If this book has inspired and helped you in any way, help others by sharing your experience and this book with them. They will be glad you did!

ABOUT THE AUTHOR

Joanne Radke has been a hands-on pastor, mentor, counselor, coach, and friend for over 45 years, helping 100's of broken people from all walks of life regain their lives again.

Fifteen years in her 46 years of serving people have been spent pastoring and working with the Salvation Army, practically helping families in many different situations. She has helped many families downsize and organize their homes and lives and mentored and coached others to get their lives back on track emotionally, physically, financially, and practically. Joanne has a big heart of compassion for people and loves to help them where she can.

She has a big heart of compassion for people and has worked in six different ministries and has served in various capacities in ministry throughout Canada and many parts of the world. For the past 17 years has overseen the CBA – The 700 Club Canadian prayer center, where she trains the prayer team and ministers to many people daily by phone, across Canada.

Joanne has various expertise and has ministered, helped, and prayed for thousands of people. She was ordained in 1979 with the Salvation Army and later, in 1984, credentials with 'Emmanuel Fellowship Inc. She is also a certified Pastoral Counsellor of The Evangelical Order of Certified Pastoral Counsellors of America since 1979 and a Registered Clinical Counsellor with The Canadian Christian Certified Chaplaincy Association' since 2019. She is highly qualified to write on this subject through her experience and credentials.

Joanne has always loved writing and has published many articles in various magazines and ministry pamphlets. Her heart is to get the saving and healing gospel of Jesus into all the world.

OTHER BOOKS AND MATERIAL BY JOANNE RADKE

FOR CHILDREN:

Jessica The Dreamer - CD Audio Book - Jessica dreams of ice cream, rivers, and banana boats and what she wants to be when she grows up. A fun book that will teach your child to dream big and know that they can be whatever they want to be with God's help.

FOR ADULTS:	**Bible Study Training**
Intercession Series:	5 Lessons on Prayer
Hearing the Voice of God:	9 Lessons
Mining for Gold in God's Word:	10 Lessons
Pillars of Success – Godly Values:	9 Lessons
Power Gifts – Spiritual Gifts:	9 Lessons
Spiritual Root Causes of Disease:	9 Lessons
The Courts of Heaven:	9 Lessons
Victory through Prayer:	9 Lessons
Who is Our God Jehovah:	9 Lessons

To purchase any of this material, just visit: www.Declutterin30Days.com

WERE YOU BLESSED?

If you were helped or blessed by my book, would you do me and our future readers a huge favor? Would you take a minute to write an honest review for them to read? It is quick and easy to do!

I would be so incredibly grateful; it will remind me that my labor in writing and putting this book out was worth it all. Thank you again so much!

Just visit the link below, and it will take you directly to the right page:

Review.Declutterin30Days.com

Thank you so much for doing that. It really does mean a lot to me as a new author. When you share your great comments about how this book has helped you, it will help others to see the great value in getting this book and reading it for themselves. If it has motivated and helped you in your home, it will help others when they read your review. Thank you once again for your time and sacrifice to do this. It does mean a lot.